MAD WOMAN

Diary of a

MAD

WOMAN

By:

Angelica Warner

MAD WOMAN

DIARY OF A MAD WOMAN

Copyright © Sherry Phillips

Printed in the United States of America

ISBN-13:978-0692364437
ISBN-10:0692364439

Printed by Createspace 2014
Published by BlaqRayn Publishing Plus 2014

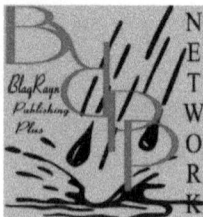

MAD WOMAN

Diary of a

MAD

WOMAN

By:

Angelica Warner

MAD WOMAN

This book is in Dedication To my God Father

I would like to dedicate this first book of mine to my biggest Inspiration in life.

Some one who made me feel that there was one person in this world that knew exactly how I felt, but more importantly that I was not all the things that they said I was.

Through his poems, music, writings, quotes, and Art; God used him to transform my mind, and soul. He is an incredibly important person in this world, and his work has been see all around the world.

" If everything in your life is a Lie, then live your best lie. As long as you live your best lie you can only hurt your self."

-Marilyn Manson.

MAD WOMAN

Dear Brian Warner,
With out your work there would have
been no impact on my life. With out
this impact I would be dead today from
Suicide. I thank you, and admire you
for all your hard work, and dedication
that you put into everything you do.

If it was not for you, I would not have
found the meaning to God in my life...
Because of you I am a true Believer in
God. And where I am today with this
First book of mine. I am truly and For
Ever Grateful To a very special Man
and a Woman who will be loved and
missed by Many. Your Mother: Barbra
Warner, and also to your Father Hugh.

Love Always Angelica Warner.

\mlm/ Lady A.

Introduction

Diary of a Mad Woman is my real, raw emotions and the perception of how I saw my world on a day to day basis... Through the process of this book, I have lost Anger, I have lost Hate, I have lost all the negative things that people used to say to me..I have lost Depression and Sadness, And I fought My inner demons, and Satan, my Friends, is Real, and is a power and principle of the conditioning of the World we live in... Through this book I battled him and I won!

Who am I?

Freak is my style, Eccentric is my flavor. Love isn't a game, Angel is my name. I am the sweetest woman you will ever meet, and I will sweep the world off it's feet. Piss me off and you will get to meet the Monster inside of me. I am good at being Good, I am even better at being bad. But you will never see any thing but Class. Women go ahead show your ass! Because by the end of the night, if you don't get the shit right. I will leave this bar sporting your man like a King on my arm. I am the Queen of the night. I don't like to fight, but keep talking that shit I will make you look like the stupid Bitch that you are. 182 IQ, and trust I will use it on you. Back off my boy because you don't know him, hell you have proven you don't even want to have a reason too. Bottom line ladies, Men like class. So shut your fucking mouth before I make you look like the ass we already know you are. This is to All the so Called Drama Queens, you already know who you are. Lady A is stepping in so Get out of my fucking Yard!

Chapter One:

All My Hate and Pain

No bad mood

Please don't be upset by the things I do or say to day. I love you to much to ruin your day I miss you greatly but today isn't my day. I just want to say I love you by leaving my bad mood out of your life today..

The Monsters in the Closet

The man that you called superficial, you are just looking at the surface of something Great. The one that you say doesn't care, or believe in any thing. Once believed but has been shown hate.

He is not this monster that you see, he is not some superficial thing. He once believed in love, and God.. Then all you did was show him hate.

He is now the man that was created by all the monsters in your closet. The monsters of the careless, and uncaring humanitarian race.

If you continue to fail to see deeper then the physical being, you will never see why his heart is breaking. There is a constant reminder of all that has been lost, a constant reminder of the lack of love, and support. This is what burns behind the eyes of the Heartbroken Man that you called A monster.

And the Monsters in the closet live inside of Me.

Suicides Mirrors

Me:

*My life once again has become my hell,
Striving every day to live a delusion, because
the lie is better then it being real...*

*I make my world where I am happy, even
though I am in pain, and in the mirror of my
life I just want to say good bye to such a place.*

*There are many who want to see me fail,
many who would love it if I take the darker
road and end it all, commit the suicide that I
think of once and a while...*

*There is nothing wrong with me, death has
been apart of me for so long. I cheated death,
and beat him once, spiritually pushed to the
brinks of suicide, and he almost won...*

*But this time I know more then I did when I
beat him before, and i have the demons of
death accompanying me on my arm.*

*I died once before, and through this life I will
die again, but what will be left of this mortal
shell I can not tell you what I see inside the
mirrors of myself...*

Myself:

*It is empty here inside, and I am merely a
vessel for all of these souls to hide. I will not
let a single person claim my life, but I can not
tell you what I see, inside of the suicidal*

mirror of me...

It is dark and sinister, and it has nothing to do with me...

It came from all the people that have hurt me, all of those that carried on and have made a mockery of my name, to those are all the people's souls that I will claim...and they are waiting in my mind, to take over just one time.

Me:

And all the souls waiting to devour me, for they are the suicidal mirror that is untold in the mind of a woman abused...and they tell the lies that I am so used to hearing...

The Demons Speak:

You are not good enough to be...

Why are you here no one loves you, no one cares...

The I:

The bitching and moaning of all the mortal sins I have done, all the pain that I have caused.

The Demon Speaks

Your wasting your time with your life, your life isn't worth the time it will take to grow up...You were never good enough to be so why don't you just take my hand and end it all with me???

MAD WOMAN

My Self:

These are the whispers of the demons in my suicidal mirror, called the mind and i fight.

Because I will be damned if I am going to let the people who hated me, and hurt me win.

I would rather live and go through hell....Then to give satisfaction to the ingrate people who want to see me dead

Me:

I have a bad attitude? I am the Bitch? For give me for Being the things that you hate, but as I recall it was you that made me this way.

My Self:

I am the woman that every one fears, but in the end l am a product of my environment , and people made me the way I am, and I will over come the suicidal mirror, and become the demon inside of me that wants to see me dead.

I:

It isn't really my life that the demons seeks, but they have come to claim the lives of the weak..

My Self:

I beat the demons in my mind once, and i will do it again, and in the end I will feed the weak to the suicide demons inside the mirror of me.

Me:

MAD WOMAN

This is the end of my demise, and the beginning of the end of your life...I am done with people who don't give a shit about me, and the suicide Mirror is now where I hide.

The Demons inside:

I am lurking and waiting for some one like you, some one weak to take your life away from you. To turn the tables of your own mind against you.

This is the beginning of the end not for me But for you.

You will never be loved, you will never have what you seek, you will never have the chance to be. You are nothing but a freak. It will all be okay if   you just take my hand and end it all with me???

My Self:

These are the whispers, and the lies of the demons inside of my Mind.

The suicidal mirror, and i fight for my life!

Because I will be damned if I am going to let the Demons win. I would rather live and go through hell....

Me:

Fuck all the people that made me the Freak.

I will live to see you die in Misery.

MAD WOMAN

Note to those who don't understand:

I hope that this poem helps people to understand that the Depressed and Suicidal are not Freaks of Nature Nor are we the Weak.

We are actually stronger then those who do not suffer in their own minds. For whom can understand the attack of the Mind better then one who has been through it and seen all the things that the Mind can do.

The Mind is a powerful tool, and it can be used against yourself and others. Be careful what you say to the Tormented Ones, Because you Never Know if it is you that will cause them to take their lives.

Note to those that Suffer

I am a suicide Activist, I have suffered from Depression from the time I was four and Raped, and through out my child hood to the Parents that raised me. Straight into my teenage years from all the bullies I wound up beating up in school, Through my Young Adult hood To the people who never understood. People are the demons that use their words to Kill the spiritual nature of people like me. To me that is Demons, all the people that strive to Make the lives of others Hell...Demons to me are all the people who turned my mind against me. Just with the power of their words.

Razor Blade

There is an emptiness in my eyes this morning and the sorrows of the past are flowing, through my mind and my body. No signs of last night's depression except for the scars of a Razor blade across my arms, and the emptiness will soon float away, only to return with your soul another day then once again My arms will be scared with the strokes of a razor blade.

Written in 1992

MAD WOMAN

I remember Every Thing

*When there seems no reason to live no reason
for you to be here and the pain becomes to
much to bear. Believe that you are here for a
reason and that you are loved by me. I can see
the pain behind the sarcasm of your jokes,
and I can see the dust of fallen memories. I
can see you trying to remember your own
fucking name. You have loved and cherished
but who has given you the same.*

*Yes its so much easier to give up on loving
you...but my heart my soul won't let you go,
and I sit here waiting for the day when I can
return home to you. When I started my
journey I knew that where my heart is there
would be you. Despite what people think is or
is not good for me. I will always chase the
dream of finding you and setting us both free.
I want you to know you are valuable to me.
And I will die trying just to get back to you.
For I remember every thing.*

*To the one my soul Loves: Justin Alan
Longwell*

Null and Void

*You call me a monster, and you wonder why,
why I am so cold and heartless on the out side,
Actions speak louder then words so why
should I continue to try...Now I am not
responsible for the actions I take,the truth is it
wouldn't matter if I tried to care, or if I
pretend that your simply   are not there...My
action's good or bad at this point isn't a factor
it's null and void...The truth to the matter is I
Don't know why I continue to take it...*

*I must like the torture that I continue to go
through, I don't even know why I like it but I
must to keep on putting my self through the
nine circles of hell, just wanting to be me, and
be set free... But it doesn't matter how I feel
because your to selfish to care....So all that is
said or done is null and void....My thoughts
are done.*

<u>*Regrets*</u>

My memory is sharp as a knife, every little thing you said or did I can play back in my mind. Sometimes I wonder if its a curse, but then I look back and realize I'm glad I remember. I hold it all inside, good or bad it never dies...it sits there dormant, like a time bomb. I can't help the things I hide. Simply because my words are weapons that can scare you for life...People call me quite.

I sit here and listen to the shit mother fuckers say... Gathering all the facts before I throw it all away, but when the facts come out you will regret every thing. I'm not a genius, but I am not stupid or innocent to the thing I have heard and seen. Underestimated from day one... hell yeah that's me. I am not an asshole by nature but when it concerns lies and deceit trust me in the end nothing can be hidden from me. Even the sweetest Angel carries a demon inside, and soon I will not be able to hide the anger in me...Keep pushing me around soon u will see. It will be you who will regret everything.

MAD WOMAN

F U and a C K 2 !

It took 3 days for Christ to die. Died for the world, but was that a lie. He may have died for you, but He never died for me. Always putting the nails in me. Every day that I have spent in this world has been a day in Hell. Your dyeing God man if he would have died when he was high and just for me, he wouldn't have left me in such a desolate ignorant place. With all this inhumanity. He took my prayers and turned it into a fucking night mare. So I put on today my F U and a C K too, and I build a new God to medicate my ape. Murderers are murdering the pretty souls every day and walking away free...till the murderer becomes me. Suicide isn't murder if these fucking mindless apes drive you to be dead inside any way! When I'm God all my murders will pay.

You can drop the S because you always said I am an Ant. However when I get done recreating my world. I will watch you, and you will see I will be the fucking Hail Mary. Give me your drama and I'll be the Queen. No one promised me the world so today I take it by force with an F and a U and a CK too. Because I am a fucking Saint to deal with some one like you.

Open doors

The more I sit back and think of you, I realize that I am alone amongst bad company. The humans around me haves forgotten who I truly Am.

And I keep praying to see your face, go ahead I open the door to you and where you are is home. I walk through the door in my mind. It gets lonely here on earth some times and my spirit has found your fountain of youth, but it has run dry. So I have come to replenish you. No one believes in you any more, But where you are is home, and I rest in you. Its getting harder to finding that Yin to my yang. I feel your soul when I'm under your halo and I hear you calling me home. To the closet in my mind.

The only place I can seem to find the one that loves me deep inside, and I wonder will die Missing you?

Out of the Dark

Don't try to hide the dark for out of Chaos came love, knowledge, wisdom and understanding. We who love the dark understand this, so there for we like the darker sides of life! But don't judge us for even tho we love the darkness there is a tremendous light inside, that if u look hard enough u can see the stardust sparkle in the sun light!

U knew it was going to get a poem out of me Son... Because I see you shine and u are Bright!

To my God son Raven Crimson from Norway.

Trying to Let go

I will always hold on to the the dreams I had, and the love i felt for the time I had it...I don't know what the future holds, but I know that going with my gut feelings have never failed me...

I don't want to hurt you And I don't want you to hurt me...They say when one door closes another opens: I will never forget you and all you have done, and you will always be in my life...

But as for this love of mine I have to Bury it...

Because even though I loved you, You never Loved me. Even though you will never tell this to my face, The heart does not lie. Some things are better left unspoken, and I will cry to the Skies.

Repent

The tolerance of humanity has put our world in a dark place, our overindulgence of this not needed greed caused us to be cast into the darkness. The revelations don't you feel it coming..more destruction will we be hold as mother earth takes her wrath and show us her darker side, our suffering to find away home is just another way to die... There could be no other reason why we fight, we should have seen this coming,

we are the warriors from the sky..sent here to watch over mankind, but they pollute your rivers,land and sky, can we repent in time, its just another way to die...

the time bomb is ticking but no one is listening, mother earth calls out in devastation, now the end is coming ...there could be no other reason why...the numbers to the revelation is coming, we that came from the sky we are rising... and the millions cry out to be saved but for us it's just another way to die...

inspired by Five finger Death punch.

MAD WOMAN

Depression's Voice..

In my deepest darkest depression, The fear and pain consumes my heart..There is no one on this earth that understands the conditioning of my mind that has been created by man...

Depression's voice.
(I am never good for any one, nor will they care what I have gone through, I am an empty vessel, a hollow shell, a mere mortal in the eyes of all men. A mechanical Animal.)
And even thou I am a broken piece of potters clay, and because I get depressed some times, doesn't mean that I can heal, it just means it's gonna take time, but there is the depressions voice in my head that is always in the back of my mind..

It is the voice of all the people that has left my soul dead and burned from the hells that are left behind. And it is unfair that some times I just don't know how to get ride of all the doubts that were left behind..
But I am a new person now and I understand that God has taken this vessel and has broke me down, not to serve man, I was here to serve the Potter that made me who I am, and in the end if I can help those along the way to understand that there is no need to feel that there is no hope and that some one does love

them then I have done my Job.

What I want and my dreams are irreverent for not all people are meant to find love , But all people were meant to be loved.

Defeated

There is nothing left to say.
My eyes are filled and my mind is blank.
I tried to talk to someone I thought who cared
but it is clear that the only one that loves me is
the same God that gives me the pain and the
tears.
There is no more reason to complain, no one
truly cares but him anyway..
What does it matter any more to an unbroken
soul...
What the unbroken heart hast to say...
But I have to live through this pain,
Just to find and meet my twin flame..
Where is the soul that will never leave.
Feeling all alone and defeated.

<u>Chapter Two:</u>

Trying to Break the Cycle of Abuse

Breaking Chains

My Self Talking to Lucifer:

Okay Karma. You want to fight me for your right to create chaos and Hell in my life. Come after me because you know I battle well, and I am some one that doesn't take your shit sitting still.

There are many souls I have set free in the course of all my pain, and there are many souls you try to clam just like me and your pissed because the endless contracts that you get these souls to sign, I break every one of them. Breaking the Chains of the Demon called Suicide.

Every one of your demons you send after me I send them back to Hell and for that you hate me. Your contracts that you make are endless words empty and all in Vain.

Because I am the Lady A, and I use your passion of hate, to set my people free. Lady A is coming, and Damien too. You can't play any more games with me.

I am the Hail Marys too, and I rule over you. Lady A Breaks all your eternal chains bringing about positive change.

Sending all your demons back   to hell. You might be part of God in the shady Grey, But I

*am God too, and So much bigger then you...
RUN and be very Afraid. I will have freedom
and I make no deals with you. Remember my
Name.*

*I am going to Bringing Zion to me, and I ask
you father dose it kill you? That you made
one as powerful as Me?*

*Fuck your evil and your lies...Breaking
Chains. For all to survive.*

Victims aren't We all?

I looked to the Angels, when I became insane..I looked to the voices that was in the back of my brain. Some where there I found a guiding light of love and spiritual delight. And there was nothing that wasn't in side of me that is not a part of me..

Bi polar is a diagnosis they give to the em-path that feels the emotional distress of other people.

Schizophrenia is the diagnosis that they give to God's saints.

And the world has these people thinking that there is something wrong with their minds today.

Where was medication in Salem? Where Was the medication when the mass hysteria of the Catholic churches was burning the witches??

Would you have called the Pope a schizophrenic sociopath when he tied a little girl to a bed to bring the devil out of her? And what happened to that little girl? She was killed in a exorcism..

You tell me is it fair that you have these people's minds thinking that their evil?

Is it the people that are evil these days or is it the doctors that are working for the government? You tell me who the victims are...

Victims aren't we all???

MAD WOMAN

So many tears

Where do I run to when my cup is full?
Where do I hide when I am scourged...
Where is the salvation of my refuge
to hide inside the one I love when I am in
pain...
I am the Angel that has held all the pieces
together for so many, but I am the Angel that
holds in all the tears for the twin flame...
And if I cry, and shed a tear, it rips the hearts
out of the ones that I try to save...
This is why I don't cry in front of those that I
love, and care for because they can never
stand to see me shed any tears anyway...
And there is only one who understands my
tears, and only one who can save me from the
pain...
But is is quite clear that he isn't here and I
feel left all alone, and empty inside...

And I asked Christ, What is the point to life if
I must live it all alone...To Die.

Crucified

*Does anyone understand what that feeling is
when there is an abyss in the the heart of a
man looking for the twin flame...
To have a hole so deep inside that all you want
to do is die...And we are crucified every night
my love for we have lost the flame..
It is forbidden they say to take a life even if it
is your life that you take..
So we as men take the power of life and death
out of our hands...
And we understand that no matter how
painful it is to go on with out the one we
love...
It is a blessing to be alive...
So we strive to thrive.
But we have to endure the pain till the
end..and it becomes so strong of a hold to
death that it is even hard to let God inside..*

.

*For who would want to deal with some one so
weak that all we can do any more is cry*

God's nature

*There has been so many doubts and fears
inside my mind... that it is hard sometimes to
find peace in the soul of all man kind...
And at this point we are all struggling to find
the same...Infinite love and light..
God is a million different things, some times it
hard to find some one who knows the roles
and many sides...It is not for a common man
to know the all the sides to God..For even
man does not know all the sides to
himself...Only when man understands the
nature of the soul with in himself...
Will he understand God in the flesh that died
to save our souls from Hell...*

Worst Fears

So many times I have wondered when will death come to claim me?? How much time do I really have left on this earth, and how long the heartache will last?

And I fight the pain of suicide daily and if it wasn't for my twin flame I would not even care to stay. If it wasn't for the love that he has shown me, and the love that I have always felt from him, I would have taken this life along time ago...

But it is the drive of his love that keeps me here.

And so I live for my King, because I don't want you to have to live with out me, Just as I don't want to live with out you.

And though I miss you all the time, and I feel that we are running out of time...

I am aware that you are here and I am with you in the winter of our worst fears and together I know that we will get through, the winter of our discontent.

Where is home?

Home is where you are in the presences of all souls in the company of many different faces, from different times, places, and races.
In the short time that I have spent with you on this Journey, through this life I seek your face, and your face alone. So that you can show me the Grace and Mercy of your love in this empty place we call home... The Earth.
Some people will love me, Some people will hate me,
Some will understand me, and some wont. Some will listen and enjoy the words I have to say, and some will turn me away. My Father just as they did Yahweh. Those who understand will seek my face, From some eventually I will just have to walk away. For it is better to love all people as a perfectly imperfect person and to walk away with love in your heart, then to fight and struggle to love some one that isn't where you are...
But as long as I love you, and am Faithful to you, I will face all my days on my journey through the wilderness and will love every one I came across because you first loved me.

Spared

I am a battle born soldier, Not self made, not self proclaimed, but Shining bright because I refuse to let the darkness in you Bring me out of my light.... You see I faced this Demon before, the one that took apart of me that just doesn't care what you think any more, and I will not let your prosecution destroy my heart. I don't know where this Journey ends but I know that I am not apart of that world any more and I refuse to be.

Once I had an open point of view before I had a clue, and I have stood alone for so long, but I know this now That I am never alone, and My God is the warrior in me, that will defeat this life, even unto death, and there at the Judgment seat when he calls me out by name, I will not relay on my works that I have done, but I will stand firm in his name, and I will be spared from people like you

MAD WOMAN

The Angel of the Demons...

Eventually The voices in my head will go away, And there will be nothing left for me to say.

Till that day comes I will burn the quills of the pen to those things that I have to say.

My words are like weapons and that can cut like a knife, I will pierce the hearts of all the men that took my life.

This sinner that you thought I am, has become the saint that never would have been, if it wasn't for all their hate. What else could I say in a world full of hate, It was not the one true God that I despised but the God of all the people that I hated and I wanted to see them die.

So now I turn all the hate around on all the haters of my life, and I light a candle for the sinners, set the world on fire for the ones that I want saved.

And in the end they will be saved, because I fight to send the demons back from where they came..

The Angel has become the demon that the demons hate..

Some one... To No One But You

*Yesterday I was dirty, and there was no hope
to save my soul. Today I am white as snow,
and covered in the blood.*

*And the isolation of this world is an oxygen
mask to the ones that are trying to survive the
passing of every day human events.*

*I am not a slave to a god of man that says that
I am a nobody, nor am I a slave to a person
that doesn't care to see that I am a
somebody...*

*But Trust and believe I do work for some one,
and it is not this world.*

*I work for the Greater Good, and I will deal
with all the Bull Shit of the world just to make
sure that I am not forgotten on this
earth...and that my people are not forgotten
too...*

*I am not perfect, and I am not a Christ, I am
not a Saint, but I promise you all that you will
see Good or Bad in me is of God... 100
percent reality.   For out of the darkness I
saw the light, and out of darkness I came.
Because I know not to render evil with evil
and turn the other cheek so shall I be hid in
the the shedding of the blood, and as Zion I
will be hid from thy face for all eternity...*

MAD WOMAN

Sands of Time

Damien speaks:
Some where in the sands of time I got lost and
could not find a way out of the prison inside
my mind.
Locked inside Pandora's box I was lost, alone
and scared...
Then Pandora found me and helped me
through my worst fears...
She told me all the things that the devil's
could do, showed me all the things that he
would use against me,
And gave me the tools I needed for Victory.
The worst thing in the world is where the
demon's dwell, inside dormant in my mind.
Lost some where in the sands of time.

Trying to break free of the pain, the hurt, and
all the regrets...
Is there any thing to this mortal shell that is
left? Or am I just an empty vessel?
And in the end there was one thing left.
One thing that Pandora gave me that no one
else ever did, And left me with a Mark that
had no sin...
She showed me love, and gave me hope...
And that is what makes her my guardian
Angel over the monsters inside my mind...
For it was and is with in her power to take
them away and set me free...For she alone has

MAD WOMAN

*the Key to Damien's Box, And there is so
many of us that grieve to be set free...
This is my Prayer to thee:
Hail Mary..daughter of Eve.. Rise up and give
the lost and fallen hope..
The sons of Adam are in great need...
And the Angel of Men the Mary Magdalen
came to us to for fill his will and set the
children of Cain free... Hail to the mother and
the Queen...
Amen*

MAD WOMAN

Unkillable Monster

*There is a Monster inside his mind..
Telling him that he is a devil, uncaring
and unkind. Making him crazy.*

*In the mind of a mad man there is an
unkillable monster...To every one but
the one.*
*The one that sits on the right of the
King of Kings on earth...*

Chapter Three:

The Battle

Holy Battle

*I choose to fight for Love and peace on earth,
you will never understand my battle or my
promise of the rewards at the end of my
Journey. This is my life and my Journey to
live for Yahweh, The Father has a purpose for
me.*

*You can not see into this soul of mine because
if you could see eye to eye you would be able
to see the place where I have gone so cold..
My spirit is saved some where in Zion, and
that is where my home is...*

*So I ask God to awaken me and save me from
the wilderness the darkness of this place
where I have become comfortably numb. And
I know when I miss your presence from my
soul, that I am being Called home..*

*So I ask the Father to quicken me to life, call
my number and save me from the nothing that
they say I am for I used to be a Saint, and
soon we go marching into battle.*

Dear Zion

If you have never seen the Large Golden Eagles, then you don't know when they take flight. We are prepared and ready to turn us towards the holy city, as this earth takes it toll..

heading home to Zion where the virgins will be spared from physical death for we have paid our price and Debt to the father and taken up our crosses. The 144 thousand that will not be left behind. We are being taken and called up according to our numbers.

We are the rulers over the earth for we are the preachers, and the prophets.

Be hold how good it is for family to come together it is a greater blessing then the blessing of Aaron that went from head to toe. For the dew of the Lord is upon his Children Zion.

MAD WOMAN

Heart of Stone

Your not made of Stone and you do not stand alone.
I am not the hero but I am just a fighter for the righteous side of hell, and you my love are getting closer to the lighter side of the darkness with in you,
I miss you when your not in the spirit with me, and taking you back to your roots...I want you to crash into my soul like the speed of lightening, so that my heart will explode to where all the pieces will blow apart...and I shall be whole again.

MAD WOMAN

Feelings

Narrator:
People say that she is different, people say
that she is really weird, but people say that she
is Kind and Caring...But yet when she goes
home she is in tears.
She has prayed for love her entire life, and
she is loved by so many. Some times she
doesn't know how much she is loved or the
impact that she has because of that promise
that she will be loved one day by her King.
Some Random person:
You see her walk down the street talking to
herself as she goes by. But if you take the time
to talk to her, she will blow your mind.
She is smart in the most different of ways, and
close to God is she in the heart; but she
doesn't see him the same way as most people
do today.

A Friend:
She sees God's presence in all things, Good
and Bad.
In the lion statues, in the butterfly. In the
trees in spring, in the sun in the summer time.
She sees God in the clouds, and she sees God
in all life. She is one with God through
nature.

An On looker:
There is something about her, I can feel her

peace. Not many know that kind of peace in the middle of a busy world.

The Angel:
If they only knew what a mess I really am. If only they could understand the pain that I feel. If only they knew how I really felt.. Then every thing they thought I was would be used to judge me.
All my life my weakness became my Crucifixion.
The tears and the sorrow's, the depression is always there, but it is easier to let it die inside, and choose to be happy with life.
Then to be beaten down for crying every day of your life.   No one but one understands the sadness in me. No one understands or values the meaning of Love, friends, and Family.
They say they love you in the name of God, but then turn around and do the opposite of Love. In church they tell you love every one especially your enemy. And I say love every body is destroying the value of love for tomorrow, for today.
My sadness I have learned to cope with, and me and God fight every day.. He tells me what I need to do before it happens, but just because he promises me the love of my King on earth doesn't mean I expect it.
I go through the motions and I love like Christ would love because I have found that in my life I need that love to survive, and

many of us do.
Not just because A book told me too..
I believe in Christ not because I have to, but
because it helps to know that I am not alone
in suffering in a world that makes me feel all
alone. I don't quote scripture to every one, but
to those that need it the most.. and some times
I quote scriptures with out the scriptures
because seeds are easier to plant that way.
Some time I will quote the Buddha, or
Mohamed. Some times it is as simple as sitting
next to an old man and listening to him talk
about his life in passing.
But what I seek I shall never find. In till I hit
the gate. But if I never meet my love.
Am I good to die alone. Am I good to know
that I am the only one with out a soul mate.
No. I die every day, and I do it all alone.

Pandora's Box

It takes a special person to read between these lines. There is so much more to me than just what you see, or can perceive on the outside...Looking skin deep just under the subcutaneous isn't enough. There isn't a Person alive that can reach my core, Unless I choose to let them inside. The walls I built, the things I hide...There is one who knows me, and it's not the one I thought that would ever get inside. My fortress is a castle that has been looking for a King. Now that all my walls are gone and there is nowhere to hide, I can sit here and say I know who takes my throne. Those walls I built they came crashing down around me. My walls didn't even put up a fight, and didn't even make a sound, as Some how I managed to let you deep within side my heart that's when the walls came crashing down. Your the only one that has made it through the Hell deep inside of Pandora's Box. The Torment I carry forever with me, but where you are there is hope.

<u>*Blessed*</u>

I sit and I worry about what is going on in your world. I am left pondering if one day, I will be there to try to fix everything. It doesn't matter how it has to end, as long as you are in a better place than when we first began. I don't concern myself with things that I need as long as you are here with me this is all I need. And if there ever comes a time when you are not. Please don't concern yourself with me. I have a heart of glass and I am used to picking up the pieces of the messes that is left behind. How ever if anything beautiful came from what we have. The next time I will be better blessed.

MAD WOMAN

May God have Mercy on Your Soul

May God adore you and love you, the way you never loved me. May he bring you the comfort and mercy that you never gave me. May he accept you with open arms, despite the fact you never showed me comfort, compassion, or acceptance of the daughter that you help to create...

And out of your Hate for me I pray that he shows you mercy for all that you have done to me. At the Hour of this Unexpected death, the Hail Mary prays for your soul to remain forever at rest, and may all your sins be forgiven of you.

I accept your death and welcome it as your Karma paid in full, and as you lay in your eternal rest. I pray that he grants you peace, and rest.

May God have mercy on your soul

For my Father Herbert Lynn Phillips

Dare to Dream a little Dream...

The hope of love is endless if you know where to look. And some where out there I know that your there and my soul calls to you. The one my soul has loved from the moment our names were called. But it feels although the sands of time are running against me, and I am running out of time.

Yet I still dare to Dream a little dream of me and you. Your presence in my life, and your essence of love has awakened my soul..And your soul still lingers here in mine.

I miss you like heaven misses their prized Angel, that fell to earth to find the one her soul loves. And yes the Queen still dares to dream a little dream of true love. And I am trying to find my way home.

MAD WOMAN

Dead Man's Pass

My soul is unquieted tonight, there is nothing here to still my mind, as the memories and thoughts race, I am taken miles away to a place that stills my soul. Trying any way I can to get to you, but when I arrive all I can see is the stillness of the dead and broken memories of a place long ago forgotten. Like the tragedy of my life that seems to be but a shadow and a memory. And when I am still I can feel you. It isn't hard to see why they Call it dead mans pass. As I over look the emptiness vast plan of high grass; I feel a gust of wind and so it starts to snow. I can almost hear your voice. In the wind as if you are right here with me. Not a star in sight.

I sink into the emptiness. O my immortal comes, please bring me peace to my soul tonight. There I sit, over shadowing the memories of my life. I wonder. Therein the in between do you know how much I miss you?

There was so many questions left unanswered. So much more I wanted to say;But it seems that death wont come to take me to you to the between place. As the tears come I wonder do you still care. Where ever you are do you know how much I still need you here? And the burning. The anger, the passion. Why does she even care? How do I care for a soul?When I feel there is nothing left for me here? And I am left with the memories that I am alone. But yet I still feel you here, my immortal believe me when I say: It isn't you it really is me.. And I don't know how to be.. All the things that you see in me....And there comes a whisper of A voice I have never heard, but yet know so well... You don't have to know how to be there my love, but some how you just are..And know I am with you.

For my best friend Shaun Mason.

Impacted

*I was made in the image of not a man.. But
man took that image and made it into a devil..
There is nothing that I haven't suffered that I
have not learned from... Be it of God or of the
man that made me to be a lie.. If every thing
that I stand for which is perfect love and
perfect trust is a lie then why is it that my
enemies fall at my feet.. It may not be right
away but in time they will fall.. and My family
that was also taught these lies will come to
know truth.. the enemy is not the man alone,
but that which came from man.. But as of
God I am .. and it is given to me by the holy
spirit that I may become a ruler among men..
If you knew the God of which I spoke
you too would know that all the authority
was given to us from the moment of the
immaculate conception.. that wasn't so much
of the Mother Mary as it was the mysteries of
the heavenly father that created the two souls
from the beginning of time before the flesh
was created...*

*Do not be confused my brothers and sisters
about what it is that is putting you through
hell...It is not what you presume it to be..
Hold fast to the truth, and the love, and to the
virtues of the heart, and be of Good faith.
Watch your thoughts.. they become words..
watch your words they become actions...
Those actions can impact your life.*

Chapter Four :

The Angel Emerges...

The Eastern Star

Through it all she was my guiding light. She shines as bright as the morning star from whence she came. She knows the truth that hides in the night skies, and few will ever find the guiding love of her embrace. But for the few that find the Hail Mary's grace, They are guided to the light out of the darkness to understand that even in the night the morning star is beautiful. And through it all Till the End. The mother was there to guide their souls. There is never the purest love that was ever found, then that of the Eastern star's guiding light..And where she is there is Love.

<u>Guiding Light</u>

*You were my guiding light. The love of my life.
An Angel sent from the great sea, just like me.
And I miss u like heaven misses there Queen.
I wish I could say that this love of mine could
last for ever. But in my world it rains like in
Ireland all the time, and your affections are
far beyond my reach. But I am far beyond
driven, and to deep in my emotions to let you
go. If everything happens for a reason, who is
to say your not the king I seek. Only time tell
no lies, and your presence for ever surrounds
me and where you are I am home. Come find
me in the garden. The one before this time
and space was made. Where the forbidden
fruit tastes so sweet. And you my love are
forever special to me. Some things pass away
and change, but you and I will remain long
after death has taken hold. And our spirits
will become free when I feel you lying next to
me, and I am in your arms. You are my
wishing star I see, A true vision of ecstasy.
And I long to come home. Even if is just to see
what might becomes a bitter sweet memory.
You are my guiding light of the soul.*

MAD WOMAN

Prayers Of a Hail Mary

It has been so long since I have spoken deep words to you in the unknown deep place. It has been so long since I have connected with you in the secret places of my soul. On the astronomical plane I call home. I know that you're out there and tonight I need to speak to My King. The one who rules his own world and can shape reality into anything. Hope gets harder to hold onto every day, and it seems like the love that I shared with you my love has gotten me nothing but broken dreams. What do I hold on to when all i see around me is people suffering with pain? Is my pain any less then theirs? Is my prayers forgotten because I hide my pain to fight for others instead of my own? Is there A reason I feel that my dreams are null and void to ever becoming something true. And no matter where you are I continue to search for you. Even if I found you and come face to Face with someone so profoundly from a different time and space, I would still be just another person in passing to you; And never really mean anything to you.

For I understand now dreams are never supposed to be reached. Yet I still diligently seek for something true. Not so out of touch, but always out of reach. And I'm so lonely here without you... I just want to go to sleep. Because I find that the one I am looking for

*in this never ending dream is merely a lie to
me. For as I know all too well for people like
me and you death is just another fucking
beginning, and yet I still love you even though
I never know whom it really is that I seek. But
I know that no matter where I go my immortal
is always with me.*

MAD WOMAN

The Mason's soul

Out of every thing in my life that I have been through, out of all the experience I have seen, I can feel the darkness creeping inside of my brain. Like a rain cloud that seems to never go away.. it is the feeling of the sad and lonely that never seems to fly away, And though you will leave me my love, I am better off alone. For it is not me that I lock away, but the heart of the love that burns for that one. I am free and I gave you all the chances to love me..

But in the end I feel that I will die alone, Unhappy and unquieted in this never ending circle of love.

You said that you were happy for me, you said that you were glade I had found some one. But in the end my heart said I was a fool not to sit back and wait for you.

In the end my love if I am to remain true I have to listen to my heart and follow after you. For my heart knows that I have been captivated by the devil with in your soul. The Angel in me loves the devil in you. For I am what I am and I will always have the Mason in my Soul.

Mother Mary

She is the Keeper of the mysteries of the universe, the last and final seal to walk the earth. She eats up all the demons and devours them, and spits them out Back into the universe from whence they came.
She is a great woman of Mystery..
Where for is the great woman of the fallen?
Who cries out to Babylon?
Who will come to the aid of the Angels that are on earth to help them find their way?
There is only one, that will and chooses to break man kind free..
She is a woman of great love and Mysteries...
The one they called Hail Mary.

<u>Gates</u>

I speak what I want to see because it is in my
mind eye to see that which you can not dear to
dream...
In my soul   I carry what I   want my
destiny to be
Do not disrupt the natural flow
Man in the flesh operating on the   level as
the universe, walking with faith
You claim to be legit but your so damn blind..
I am making God run on my time...
While your sitting left behind
So let me get you in the mood take it to the
moon,
You think you know Wisdom, but your still
just acting a fool..
Look around you what do you see...
I am breaking the Matrix Code
While your still fighting to be free...
Dreams are your heroes you just haven't open
the doors
So I will be stead fast, and I will keep my
sight,
fill you with fright when I walk past you in the
night, The one that was once counseled, is
now breaking free. Eating up the demons as I
walk with power. Knowledge at this level is
overlapping the human brain   dealing with
fate making my way through the gate.

The Purpose of Life

*I am like the root of a might oak tree deeply
rooted in faith.
I am like the blossom of a rose blooming in
the morning sun.
I am the bird that flies in the company of the
wind..
I am the fire from around about me spins...
I am made of earth, I am made of water,
I was given air to breath in my lungs
And the passion of the fire the spirit that fills
me..
I am not a human being, I am a spiritual
being..
That was given a body for this reason of love,
and made a protector of all man kind.
We are created to be loved, and to love.
Until man can grasp this concept of the
purpose to life the world will remain like a
desert to those with a scorned heart.*

MAD WOMAN

Blessings Undisguised
I lift your name up in praise
I heard you call me out by name
Because your undisguised blessings
Are raining down on me.
I hear your words ,Whisper in my ears
Where you are I can hide in my fears
You are my blessings undisguised
My King I pray, make me a vessel unto your name
When I am in tears teach me your ways
Yeshua I lift up your name on high
It is your saving grace that makes me a mighty tree
Deeply rooted in your faith I am a planted seed...
I have become like the river flowing free
Because your words are like the song to my soul
In your spirit I am free So...Yeshua every day
I see your undisguised blessings
are pouring down on me on my journey home
my eyes are freed...There is no where I don't
see your face and I Thank God for reviling
your face to me

MAD WOMAN

Into your Rest

We are the diamonds the stars in the sky,
We are the children of God, and his spirit
dwells in us, and we praise him with our
palms raised to the   universe...
We are one me and Christ and I knew that we
become like one right away he is my light, and
he is beautiful...and he makes me shine to all
that see my face, for he has put his grace
upon me. The whole of my eyes   is full of
light this morning, and in me my body is his
temple and there he will dwell with me till I go
to claim my kingdom upon the stars...
And when I come to him in his throne I know
that I will be comforted with rest, for I am a
daughter of Jacob and I will Go home to the
father soon..
Father I pray that I be called up in your grace
and love and lift my spirits to your glorious
coming....
For I am ready to Come home into your rest.

MAD WOMAN

Paid my Price

*I don't waist my time trying to love some one
that I know isn't on my time wave or frame...
So I do what I got to do for Christ...
Because in time that is the only man that has
bought and paid for my sins with a price...
The price of shedding of blood in exchange
for my tears and the hail Mary's cries I have
no fear.
From the dark to the light.
I have found the Key to the universe and God
is my King. I know a lot about heaven but no
one wants to hear me speak so I wait till I get
to the gate, and there is where the Angel's will
sing....
Another prophet turned away...
Every one that thinks they are going to
heaven isn't going, a lot of people who think
they are not going to heaven will be there...
Put my soul on it and Fight the devil daily...
Watch for God his coming look to the
morning in the east where you see God's halo
rising...
In the Clouds he will arise, and shall burn up
all of the skies..*

*Touching down on a place called home, and
that is when We all shall see and hear the king
that loved us all, and has no fear...
Children of Abraham, Children of Jacob...
Can you hear the father calling
Calling the star children home??*

Chapter Five:

Love Letters To My King

MAD WOMAN

A Suit made for God

*Every one will come, To my funeral just to see
that I am not there... Just the skin of a body
left behind is all that I will be...and I will be
purged from the sins of this world and all my
works will be burnt and There will be no
where left for me to hid
On that day of Judgment I will stand in My
Christ.
Call me a Bitch and Rebel... As did the
Pharisees and the Sadducees with Christ. I
would gladly take the place of Jesus but he
cared to much to let me die...*

*Think God that I am not the person that I
used to be, that with a single thought I would
steal your breath and life from my eyes,
But Through the mercy and Grace God
taught me how to used my tongue of weapons
for the greater Good of all mankind.
And I will not fight you with words that are
not enough...
Because Faith with out works is dead and I
refuse to use the evil deeds of the mind to get
to where I want to be in life.*

To my Twin Flame

*I wonder some times if you have missed me as
much as I have missed you..*
*Wonder if you know my name deep down in
your soul...*
*I wonder if all these years if you thought of
me even if you may not have known me, and
if it*
*caused you pain the way that it has caused
me.*
*I wish you knew how much I missed you, and
the presence of your soul next to mine, or how
much I care for you...*
*Every one needs that best friend that no
matter what they know that you are not going
to leave.*
*Every one needs that lover that is deep in
there heart, mind, body and soul...*
Every one needs that twin flame...
*And my love I miss you more and more every
day that you are not in my arms.*
*And you need to know my King that I am glad
to have finally found you face to face.*

MAD WOMAN

I love you through and through
To my love, the one that is a part of my soul.
You are the one that sees the unhealthy parts
of me, from the body to the soul.
I stand before you in all my flaws...
Totally naked with no where to hide, the
scared little girl that is inside.
But in your presence and your love, you have
made me strong.
And I know that you are the one that I can
trust with all my heart, and since you are the
one my soul can trust, I give you all I can.

I know where my heart and soul is, and I
know that my heart will never lie.
And I may have had to let a lot of things and
people go...
But the one that remains true my heart has
told, and in him is where the true love lies
because God told me so.
Because only God can know....
How much I love you through and through.

The Rains of Ireland

The Woman to the Man:

As the rain of Ireland come and winter sets into my heart I feel your presence lingering near, as I walk into the great gardens of love into your arms...the great winds of October can not be stopped as the turn of the tides can never truly be captured by man.

The great moon above is full and I miss u in this winter of my discontent and I long you to come home...
My soul has been troubled for so long for the husband that I once knew and with out you my love I am weak...
****

The Man to the Woman:
In the winter of my discontent my beloved I miss my soul mate as I travel quick to flee the winters of Ireland fleeing from the love I have because I don't want you to truly see the monster me...
You thought for so long I fled from you my most precious of roses I did not mean to cut you to the quick...it is not you my love I ran from, but the deepest feeling I had for you...
And I still feel like I am not what you need. But as u continue to call my spirit home, I feel

more pain. I can feel your presence lingering near me, all you want is for me to come home...

but my heart doesn't understand how such an amazing woman can love a beast like me...
****

The Woman to the Man:

I never cared that you hid your heart from me..I never cared that you didn't know how to love the roses like me..so fragile in the way I handled you with knit gloves...for I could always see the pain behind the eyes of a man I have long known, and longed for him to be set free from the torments of the demons that he has seen...
But when you hold me in your arms you are not the monster you portray your self To be...
Behind the pain you are as the weeping willow needing a great flowing spring...
Help me love bring your soul back to life who can

understand your pain better then me?
We are alone, awakened and calling for the connection of the souls...but how do I show a man love, that has never known love?.. Set from birth to be a mighty king. Taught that love and emotions were simply a sign of weakness. Yet with me the man behind the mask of that lie faded away so easily.
****

MAD WOMAN

The Man to the Woman:

When I am with you my love I am weakened buy your presence of beauty and strength...no one could ever have loved a man like me. The man that people feared you have never pushed away or feared me.. the inner strength of a woman that dared to truly know me...and I wish I could have shown you the love then that I so strongly seen...but I weakened you.. I created all your pain.. Past and present still I hate to see you cry for me... And through the time and distance you have proven your love and loyalty... It is hard for my mind to comprehend the complexity of your soul that is strong enough to love a man that is a tyrant like me...

When I am angered by the people in this world all you have shown me was that you loved the man underneath the present state of discontent for the mindless behavior of all other human beings...and despite the love you show the man behind the man that I fear...my worst fear is pushing you away because your feelings are so deep.. and when you express your mind you make the whole world think freely...

How can a woman that is strong enough to see past the emotions of a hurt man, still grieve for me to be free...

****

MAD WOMAN

The Woman to the Man:

Perhaps in time my love you will come to understand that as well as you know me I am still so complex...you will never truly understand the forces that drive me to love a man behind the mask that every one else sees...i don't look at the outside cover but I look deep within the soul, and there I see the man I have always known..And loving you is easy when I can feel you in my soul...the one that walked next to me for so long...immortals need an immortal love..one that will not fade. I am loyal to you because I know from that man I see I was made. You are my heart, an there for I cherish the love the great spirit gave me...there is nothing left to say except I have always been with you from the day we together as a whole was made. That is why it is so easy for me to love the man no one cares to see.

MAD WOMAN

My Light bearer my King

As I enter into your Palace and stand before you I am comforted by your magnificent presence. A bold light with the strongest attraction and I can feel your embrace encompass me, holding me steadfast. Protecting me and my King underneath your Halo of grace. You are the morning star, the diamond in my sky. My inspiration of hope, and my faith in the light through the dark.

And I am changing into something greater than me...Something beautiful for all to see. And you do not judge me the way that man judges me.. you are my light bearer and I am your queen. I pray that this love of mine never fades, and it can be beautiful for the rest of my days...

Addicted to You

I am so addicted to the connection that my soul has to you. Some time is scares to me how well you know me deep inside, it like I have no where to hide. It has become an addiction. The only one I know that I can talk to, and I am never judged by you. My soul can't get enough of your loving truth. And when I seem to be coming undone from my seems,my soul runs straight to you. I have become awakened and aware. Th greatest moments of truth I find in you. And when I come undone from my seems.. I feel your arms wrapped around me.

Never Cared

I don't give a damn if this is a lie. My entire life I was lied to. I don't give a damn if this isn't a dream come true. But it is my dream to dream about you. Some dream of being the boss, and having all the cars and girls. Some dream of being rock stars. I dare to Dream of you. I just want to love someone who truly loves me. I don't want money, I don't want fame.

I don't care where I live, but I do care if I never have you. It is easy to go head and pick up the knife and say one last time...It wouldn't kill me to put those scars-on my arms once again, but I know it would kill you, and in the end it doesn't even matter. I had to fall and lose it all to realize that the only thing that mattered was I love you enough not to. I am someone that will never be meant to be loved by you the way I need to be. How ever I take life for the moment and right now you are all I need. All I can do is be there as a friend for you, and pray that in the future when I am there...you will not look at me and say. I am sorry I never Cared for you.

MAD WOMAN

Cumin out of control

I like it when u kiss my lips and pull my hair. I like your dominance with the touch of I do care. I like it when u take over. But most of all I like it when you make love to me and make me cum completely out of control. Put me over your knees I haven't been bad but I still need a beating. Rest your pelvic close to me as I take all of you inside of me. Till u go down my throat I want to hear u moan. As I beg for penetration as you and I get so close. Turn me over bent at the waist you deep inside me Yes that's my holy place. It belongs to you and you always know how to make me cum completely out of control.

Still I miss You

*Wish you were hear so I could share my bed
give a little and get a little head. Run my
fingers through your hair, and whisper in
your ears. Take me to the point of no return. I
want to feel your lips pressed against mine as
our bodies intertwined. I want to run my nails
down your back. Feel you enter me from
behind, and wrap your hand around my neck.
Screaming for you to break my back. I am
never alone this is true, your presence is
always here but still I miss you. Me you and
Jack Daniels too. Jack Daniels and Cheap
cigarettes Playing Cards and the simple
memories I can never for get, and if you go
back to 1802. On the bar still stilling in
Brian's fancy bottles is the Blackberry Wine
and Jack Daniels. The playing card on the
table to the right. They were hand painted
from the mistress on top of the Jokers Lap.
Where was her husband out of mind and sight,
away on business he had no time for a Wife.
Brian and Joker is Here, and as many times
as I told you I never loved you I lied. For Now
I wonder Why I had to marry your brother
over you. Jack Daniels and Cheep Cigarettes,
playing cards, and the simple Memories of
you I can never forget, and the deepest of my
memories of 1802 still sitting infancy bottles is
black berry Wine and Jack Daniels. Many
years I stand Pondered where is My lover*

MAD WOMAN

Joker for one more time I would love to play poker. And as I drink tonight I pour out a little liquor for My lover: Joker.

Written in 1998

Souls final Judge

I feel you in my soul my love and the pleasure of you there is pleasant to the mind. It is desires flames on fire, in between my thigh's. It is the touch of my God deep within my soul. It is the gentleman's reminder that pleasure of great things come to those who have the brightest souls, and that somewhere inside the darkness I am not alone. For when he touches the secret places he unlocks all my soul. Leading to my hearts desires of love in its purest form. That neither judge nor jury, could ever decide where our fate. For the answer to that question can only be found in the heart and the mind. And Only Time tells no lies

My heart is an Ocean

Just because I may need or want some one to Share my life with doesn't mean I will ever get it, my love I have learned this along time ago. Love doesn't last for ever for the immortal soul. My father loved me.. until he couldn't rape me. My grandmother loved me until I wouldn't listen to the Christian lies. My exes loved me until he cheated, and that is when I decided that nothing lasts for ever love no matter how hard you try. So why try. I remember everything, and every one I loose so I try not to love. But no matter how hard I try not to some times I have no choice but to love you. You wanted to know the real me. Hear I am this is me.

Welcome to my heart. Deep like the ocean sea. It is filled with pain because that is all it has seen. How ever some where dormant inside there is a hidden spring that is drawn from it's well, I will love you forever,but it's hard for me to tell you I love you. For words are just empty. It's easier for me to show it because I have been broken. Actions Speak louder then words and I don't want some one just to tell me they love me I want it to be seen not heard. How ever deep in the depth of the soul's love you can go is up to you, and in the end if you drowned in me I will save you, but you have to let me do so.

Open Hearts

The Girl:

You opened my heart with just one look inside.

Don't know exactly how, because all I did was hide.

I see now that you always had the Key,

You open my heart despite of me.

The King:

Opening your heart wasn't hard to do,

I knew exactly how, because I hide my heart to.

I seen I had the key, And I opened your heart despite of me.

Because you needed some one to care. So I thought I be the one to show you something you never knew.

The Girl:

You open my heart with truth and light, And shared your life

despite the fact that you didn't want to..

And you share your life with me the only way you know how to.

MAD WOMAN

The King:

I think I was surprised to see the things that I found inside of you,

They were a lot like me, for you did something I thought no one could do,

You taught me how to love you, and how trust you.

You open up my heart in spite of me,

and I still have things I hide from you yet you still choose to love me.

Despite what I tell you.

The Girl:

I am always going to be devoted to you,

For you know everything about me, all the secrets that I keep, And never once did I judge you and in return you never judged me.

I am blessed that I have so much of your trust, Something I am careful

not to loose, and I am thankful for every day that I know you

The King:

I know that your devoted to me, and I know how much you care,

And I know that in my life you will always be there.

MAD WOMAN

The Girl:

You are the reason I have hope every day,

You are the reason I smile the reason I cry,

and in my life I know that you will stay...

The two souls...

You have proven that regardless of who I am, And who may come and go out of my life, you will be the person I run to, because in the end regardless of How I do, Yes I still LOVE YOU.

Destiny

*We are all stars in a part of time and space,
but even if we were home we would still be far
away.. but there is the light that comes of the
soul, of the stars that are dead and gone.*

*I am not attached to your world nothing heals
the pain, not God, not time, not any thing, and
am unable to grow..*
*And the pretty people tear our works to shreds
and our efforts are better left dead, but in the
end you know you still reach your destiny and
others are left in there winter of there
Disconnect. And you my father, my love You
have stood by me even when I thought you
were not there, and I know where you are
there is Love,*
*And yet we still try to run to the edge of time
and space to recreate   a world to recreate our
future. But the time is running out and people
wont listen to simple truths..   So I move on
and continue to find the light with in me for
my King is bigger then he seems to be, and
there is a great Kingdom waiting, and I will
travel the world to get the that King that has
stood by me for 32 years, the one who knew
me before I knew my self, and I realize it is
my Choice on how I view my King, but when
your views, match with values, love, and
discernment It doesn't matter you will reach
your destiny in the end..*

Disconnected

As I sit here felling disconnected to the world that I have created One must wonder is there any reason why we feel disconnected every night...

If we choose to live our lives in hiding, which seems to be so much better then the reality world.. then one must be faced to live this life alone...

My life was laid out before my feet..
What I do think and see was predestined to be what ever it was going to be...
From the universe I came, from the stars I am..

I am no longer a bi-product made from a society of hate, but I am a bi-product of that which is reflected inside of me..In an image I too was made..

Just because I don't believe in a God the way that you see fit doesn't mean that I don't believe, and I have morals, and values, and rules that people at first sight of me will never understand..

And I have a shock value you to me that will make you hate every thing that you see about me, and I am more Christ like then the Christian's that pretend that they have a relationship with God daily...

I watch my thoughts, and the things that escape my mouth, for these thought that become words become a reflection on my life, and manifest in the form good or bad...And people fail to understand that I operate on a different level, and though most are comfortable just having the love of many, I want the opportunity to have the love of one. It took me many years to understand that the road to Saint's are a lonely one. I have many friends, and many who love me, and it took me a long time to learn that even though these people are in my life there is still detachment needed...I am thankful for every person I know.. weather the experience is a good one or a bad one ... It helps me to grow out side of my self, and understand that I am not important to any one, and no one is in-titled to care about me the way I do them.

So I sit back and I wait...
Is there the right person out there some where..
Is it worth chasing A dream, and then again now you must ask you self that if the person that you seek and speak to is it the same one that your seeking or is it another...
And if it truly in fact is another also trying to live the same lie, does it still make it a lie...
If I choose to believe that you are my King then regardless of the man you are my King...

True Immortals

*What I wouldn't give for the old legends of
the immortals, to be true. To become a Cold
heartless dead thing full of hate. to not have
to feel compassion for a race of humanity that
has none. But it's not. Being Immortal doesn't
mean we don't feel, love or pain...The truth
about immortals is this: We are more
compassionate for people who deserve it..The
ones that will not hurt us. When we love we do
so unconditionally, When we hurt we are hurt
deeply. Over time in the course of our lives we
learn to condition our emotions to be hid. We
are not cold, or cold hearted, We have just
seen things, that we hate about this world and
Our eyes to the truth is opened. It is then that
we turn to logic and reason behind every
emotion, every choice, every move we make
we do so to move forward with life, because
we suffer tremendous loss. We loose our selves
in a conditioned judgmental world. There fore
We die inside.*

*Like the changes of the human to what we
call vampires, yes we die. But death takes on
many forms, shapes and sizes. and we die
through time to be come awake to the new.*

*We loose friends, family, loved ones, and we
are left to pick up broken pieces and move ON.
I may leave many worlds behind, but in the
end I shall create a new one one person at a
time. . One Armageddon at a time, And I will*

live on..For ever..Not in the body I was given, but in many bodies...in the lives of the people that I Awaken. And I pray one day not only for peace on earth, but I pray that I can find My Immortal, and there I know where my home is..For where my immortal Lies is my safe place.

Prayers for My King

*Father you told me I was a Queen of Heaven
and earth and I asked for one thing and one
thing alone. I asked for the man that you
deemed worthy to take my hand. How ever
you told me that the man that I will marry
isn't an ordinary man. You promised that who
ever it was would be just like me, in the mind
in the spirit, and in the heart. You promised
that we would be different but be of like faith..
and all the people I love claim to be the other
side of fate.*

*I have faith that your will be done, because
how many times I have seen my self fail. How
many decisions have I made that was so
wrong for me to make.*

*That I have nothing left to show for any of the
hell I have gone through. And then I have you.
Who better to know me father then the maker.
Who better to make my soul mate then the
potter...*

*If I could pray a prayer for the perfect man it
would be over the king*

*Out of all his faults that he sees in himself O
lord.. I see a man that like me once had faith.
I see a man O God that once knew that you
were not a lie.*

*But unfortunately father the Christians lie.
Out of the most vile offenders that tell you lies
in the Christian faith. I am all religion and no
religion. I am an Imitation Christ and so is
he.*

MAD WOMAN

*If I could ask but one thing out of all that you
have told me to do in two years, and out of all
the miracles that you have showed me.
I ask you to fashion me a Man using a mold
that is already made, and take that man and
make him whole in your own way.
Even if I never get the chance to be with him
father. I pray.. show him all the things that
you have shown me, and teach him what it is
to have faith.
In a time when I didn't believe, in time when I
had no faith, you built me up and showed me,
all the glory of above.
So I ask you to do the same, Take his life and
make the change. In his mind and in his heart.
So that we may never be apart. I may not have
him in this world, but he is my King.
It might be a selfish thing to ask for him to
love me for me here in this life, so if nothing
else father I pray that he at least accepts me in
the next.
And as long as I live on this earth. I hope that
my King comes home, but if he doesn't and I
die alone.. I know I will see him in the next
sitting on my throne..*

Chapter Six:

The Ending of A New Beginning

Star Children's Calling ...

There is no need to scream at me,
You feel I disrespect you but you have been
disrespecting me.
All I am trying to do is to help you through to
the other side of your journey so that I can
continue on mine.
You see I had a debt to pay,
Karma has to be paid, so that I can get where
I am supposed to Go.
This is a journey from the past into the
present and I am traveling with God along the
way.
Don't   speak down on me like you own me...

I already know I owe you, but I do what I got
to do. I am only one person, and I promised to
pay my debts in full, I may have a lot to learn
but me and God are on this Journey alone.
You can say that you are on my level and you
can say that you know my Game, but you are
so far off my level..you can keep your frame.
But regardless I loved you for you...

Cold Mountain Water

*I see you in the darkness shining bright, and I
hear the voice form deep with in. There is
nothing sweater the the sound of your voice,
deep like the depths of the water.
It is the calming of the the presence that give
you a state of peace.
The fisher man standing on the water that
bids me to come, and helps me walk in the
middle of the storms that lie ahead. This is the
rock of my foundation and the castle to my
kingdom. No one other then you could ever
unlock my soul. And if I am light as a father I
pray that I will fly away on the shores of your
cold mountain water.*

To my Grandmother Darleen Gause

MAD WOMAN

Genocide

There is no time for Idol games,
There is no time for failure.
The time for the end has come
and as humanity we have failed.
Failed to learn remorse for the actions that we
take
Fail to learn the meaning of Grace.
Then in turn we have lost how to love one
another as we love our selves,
Because there is no love for us in a dying
world.
The true followers, and believers that know
that God is the universe with in us,
Are getting murdered, and rapped by a world
that is afraid of the supernatural minded.
And the closer we get to the end of time,
The more that they will try to suppress us
To Genocide.
First the Roman's who slaughtered the Jews,
To Hitler that did the same.
If the first two holocausts didn't shed enough
blood, Wait until the beast comes after you.
His bridal is in the blood,
and the moon is blood red.
Waiting for the Saint's to Go marching in.

This is Heaven to Me...

I spoke a poem in the heart, made a wish and closed my eyes, and deep inside I thought of you.
There was no clear defined reasoning behind what it was that I was looking for...
Other then the purest heart to come and love me the way I needed my soul to be love by no one but that Twin Flame.
From this man I was made.
I have felt so disconnected to life lately that love had became a bitter sweet memory, not an action taken, or emotion felt any more, and with out you I was drowning in myself pity.
I had it all figured out..
Now that I was close to accomplishing my Goals,
The only thing that I could see before me was my death, and I had accepted the fact that I would have to live and die alone...
But then you came back to me, and reminded me Why I loved, and Why I loved you..
There was no bitterness there, no animosity no shame. There was simply two souls who loved one another, they way they were never loved, and in the end it made them a stronger human being, to love that person imperfectly.
There is no one right way or wrong way to love as long as your intentions are true.
And that is why I love you...
Because no matter what through it all you

loved me with good intentions...
And that is why I love you with all my heart,
and I give you trust over all my intuitions.
If it is not right for me, and that is your
opinion I have to accept it as a part of my
inner self and not just a separate part of me.
And it is hard to trust some one with all you
have, because its all that you have left, and
Restarting over again is not an option.
I didn't expect you...
You completely took me by surprise,
You are my King my light....
It is good to know that rest is coming...
For it has been a long Journey..
The next life is a long one with you.
And I am looking forward to the Change...
To have a quite life... And to live each day to
understand that this life is not always what it
seems to be.
The imagination of the mind can create any
thing, and out of nothing this world had to
offer me was love, Yet amazingly I still found
it...
This is Heaven to me..

I give You all of Me

On this Day I give you the key to my heart, I give you the reigns to my life, and I accept the fact that we are as one soul, in one being. Separate from one another, yet of the same flame..and out of you I knew that I was made...
You are my Son of God, The Son of man and you are my light in the dark and you completely me.

And it is on this day I give you control over my life, and I I will love you through out the rest of my life, and I give you all of me as your wife...
We are going to be challenged, and we are going to fight, but if we remain true not to give up on one another then we will have accomplished what most men and women never do.

And I am ready to remain completely Happy forever with you...
In the stillness of the dark I can feel you with me. I am no longer alone on this trip, and I can always feel you with me..
There has been times through the years that I wondered...Would I ever find you.

And here you are before me.
The mind is a powerful thing, and you can accomplish anything, but remember when you

MAD WOMAN

shape your dreams, They are not always as they are seen...
But in the end it will be exactly what you prayed for...

Passion's Kisses

There is an emptiness between my secrete
places, and there is where I call my
home...and it is there that you and I were once
created in a womb. There was a separation
between me and you, and though I could feel
you with me..
I felt so all alone.
The enmity that   was put between us form
the day that we were not created but the day
that we were born...
And the secrete places are all the parts that is
missing to heart and it ranges from physical
to mental to emotional...
A complete connection, but feeling like the
connection is complete..
If we are supposed to follow blindly to see
perfection I tell it is truth all the time.
No the world is not perfect, How ever one day
it will be my perfect world..
The answers are not always hidden,
Some time it shines in the brightest of Nights.
It is like passions kiss in it's purest form.
To feel submerged into every sensation at one
time is an indulgence to my soul
And I am drowning in you but I am floating
through the obstacles life has throne me.
I am thankful for every one...
It lead me to one of the Smartest Men I
knew...
And I hope one day my dream come true.
You see the vision isn't as important as

following your heart to a desired Goal..
And trusting that God will get you through.
I give you all my reigns, and give you all
control.
I may not always be the Idol submissive but
trust I will be submissive..Some Things are
better left unseen and heard.
But at the end of the day I know that I am
going to make it through because like me you
are an Angel, even if no one else see it but me.
Take my hand through this life,
Mold me and shape me.
I am not perfect, but I am perfection in a
bottle.
If you put in the time and love, I will give you
my life in Love and loyalty.
I will always do my best to give you complete
respect, because I would never want you
disappointed in me...

And I promise to honor you as I do honor the
Father. Who are above us,   This is his vessel
that he created: and in him I find you.
For I understand that true love is loving an
imperfect person perfectly, and True love is
two that refuse to give up on one another, as
the Father who are in heaven will never give
up on us.
And in him I give you my all in All..
Because I love you.

The Alpha and The Omega

In the end of it all I followed my heart, to find that future with the love that I have always known. At one point my life was a lie, and my best lie was to become the Mrs. Manson that I wanted to be. How ever in the course of my Journey to becoming now that which I am I can see...

That I was never meant to be your Mrs. Manson

I was only meant to be that which in a way you did create me to be. I live my best lie the best way I knew how. I followed my heart, to the end of it all;

And it is true. To live your best lie is the perfect antidote to finding out your future and who you were meant to be, Because as long as you have to take responsibility for your self it all becomes quite clear...

Eventually it becomes easy not to have to depend on any one, but you. Through you I have become the woman that I feel I always should have been.

It took a lot of changing, and it took a lot of blind faith, but in the end through you I found him, In all his glory.

I always loved you, from the first vision I had of you, through the years of all your work. And in my most dire of needs my Saint came to me, and saved me from the world that I have now left behind. There are still scares,

*and there always will be. You were my Lover
and Teacher through it all. You were my safety,
and my Sanity.
I can never repay to you all the things that
you have done for me...And you never met me.
If there was one wish that I could make,
that would be tangible in reality...
I hope one day I get to shake the Hand of the
Man that help to shape my world into reality...
You see for me this book started with you
So to me it is only Fair that it ends with you.
And I know that   I will always have my
Brian with me...for I carry you in my heart
every day.
Your Hail Mary*

MAD WOMAN

To my Readers:

Thank you so much for going through this
Journey with me that has transformed my life
from out of the Madness of my own mind.
I want to thank you all for taking the time to
read these collections of poems,
That to me is more like a Diary of my life of
the past two years.

Other dedications

To: Matt Yates:

A Facebook Friend that lead me in the right
direction to do all the things I have achieved.
The First Male influence after my Greatest
fall to make me believe that life was
something Special.
He is an dedicated Solder who survived,
An Incredible Artiest, and A Dear Friend.

To Shaun Johnathan Robert Mason.

I want to thank my best friend in my life that
also inspired me, and kicked me in the ass for
two years of my life to achieve this goal, and
many more In my life. You are my best friend,
and my greatest supporter. To the man that
stood beside me damn near every day for two
years, Thank you.

To Kim Gill :

Thank you for allowing me in your home, and

MAD WOMAN

life
In a difficult and Trying time for us both. If it wasn't for you I would not be where I am today on my journey called life.

And Lastly To: Mark and Mellisa
Thank you for allowing me not only into your home, but into your Family as Well. We may have had our differences, but through this experience at your home, I learned to become a Woman, and Found my Faith completely.

To those that have passed Away

My Father:
You said That I could do anything, but then held me back from a future to every thing... So today I became A Star...It was because of you that I felt I would be a nobody..But to day I am a some body. Thank you for never believing in me.
It gave me faith to believe in my self. I still love you.

To My Grandmother:
You judged me every day I was growing up..but when I came back and found God..your judgments almost caused you to loose my love... and you apologized for all the

*things that you said. Despite the Hell you put
me through I still found God... but not
because of you...You were the reason I knew
the Devil...But Thank you for showing me
how to battle well.
And in the end you know I loved you.*

Dear Grandfather Jack Gause:
*Through Nana I learned all that you knew
about God, and I understand, why you are the
way you are.. very quite. Thank you for
teaching Her.*

Dear Nana:
*The only woman that ever deeply and truly
expressed how much she believed in me and
constantly told me how smart I was...
I hope I make you Proud.*
*" You have a better head on your shoulders
then all my girls." 2009*

To all My Angels:

*My dearest Children:
Brentny N. Wyatt R. Dannie A. Norrah J.
Savannah Hull, and Raven Crimson:
You are all special people, and I love you all
so much. No matter what people may tell you,
I love you all, and you are apart of me, and I
am a part of you.. Just because some one calls
some one something does not mean that is*

what they are.
I am not Crazy, so Don't ever let what others
say about you change your heart and soul...
Each one of you are incredibly smart and
talented.. in your own way. Don't waist your
time in life make sure you do it right the first
time, and do it better then me. Stay in
School...
To my Kings and my Two Queens:
Wyatt Riley , Dannie Angel Jr. , Brentny
Nicole, and Norrah J. Rayven...
You are a prince's and princesses, and my
King's and Queens upon this nation.. you are
my prophets ...learn about God, and Go
preach!

To Those Searching For Truth

A mans mind is most at Ease when he knows that his mate stands his mate stands next to him in all that he tries to achieve.

In all things that are worrisome, take it to the creator, and drop it at his feet; Let him shape your worries into your dreams.

Men are by nature are stressed creatures of the earth because our survival depends upon the labor of men, and they are also cursed by sins of the world.

Just as creation depends on the labor of a woman to bear all things, and through creation of life we see our future.

The Divine Meaning of Christ:

The creator became the created: And out of his own image he made God, both male and female:

The divine Revelation of the meaning of God: So at that moment when the thought was made, and the word was spoken, At that moment God was made in the spirit, and that spirit was both Male and Female.

The double Creation in the spirit

At that moment that the word became a living soul,

(Angels)

And they were both made male and female. Then it came to be that God had not caused it to rain for their was no man to till the ground. And he had a mist come up from the earth,

MAD WOMAN

And formed man from the dust in the Ground,
And breathed life into him,
A living Soul.

The Divinity of Christ:
In the beginning was the Word, and the word
was with God, and the word was God.
And Man became that which God created
before him:
A living soul.

The Original Adam:
Adam was the name of the Soul that God gave
to the flesh of a living being: The name Adam
simply means Man:
And the word became flesh and dwelt among
us:
Both times the perfectness of nature was
created,
They both became flesh. To the Father Adam,
to the son of Christ... Man was made flesh
and lived on earth, In sin.

The Double creation:
Mary's divinity Reveled:
Hail Mary full of Grace.
Just as creation depends on the labor of a
woman to bear all things, and through
creation of life we see our future. - Cathrin
There was not one perfect being but two:
And he made them both male and Female.
And Man searching for a mate could not find

the one kindred that he was looking for.
So God Caused Adam to fall into a deep sleep.
And from the bone of man, God fashioned
him a Women...
And Adam said:
This is now bone of my bone and flesh of my
flesh.
Because tho came from man you are woman.
Wo- Womb- Life bringer.
Man- Life giver.
And he made them both in the Image of him
self.
And at the moment God created Eve,
Which means mother of all life,
He created the twin flame in the flesh, and
they were soul mated into one being.
Mother Mary full of Grace the Lord is with
the:
Mother Mary through her blood line, also
belonging to King David: was the "Holy
Grail"
The blood line of a daughter of Eve.
And she was that which Christ was,
A pure being. A Virgin married unto God.
The Angel (another created being of soul's
less then men servants of God)   Gabriel
came to Mary,
and said bless are thou amongst women,
and blessed is the fruits of the Womb"
She was found to the the purest of souls,
among the living, making her divinity the
same as Jesus in the flesh,

MAD WOMAN

And he made them both male and female.
This is bone of my bone and flesh of my flesh.
At his birth, The Word became flesh again,
and dwelt among us:
This would be the second coming of the
original Adam: Man- life giver.
Jesus Christ
The Divine revelations of Jesus Christ's
Finished work.
For God so loved the world that he gave his
only son, that who so ever believed in him,
Shall not perish but have ever lasting life.

God, Yahweh- I am at the moment he spoke I
am
Became a living soul, and that soul was Jesus
the creator, in the spirit,
That dwells inside of all men through Adam-
Man.
Son of man.
At the moment of his death he was offered up
as one blood sacrifice, to atone for them all.
If at any time you have seen me, you have
seen the father. For I and my Father are one.
The creator in the spirit of Man
-Son of God
No one comes to the Father but by me:
I am the way the truth and the life.
No one can under stand the divinity
of creation and life, unless they first
believe in me, because I am the way to
the truth of Who I am.

MAD WOMAN

Which is God
This is the divine revelations given to me by
the holy spirit. Thank you for the
understanding.
-Amen.
May this be the foundation to all who seek
God in their life.

And Last but not least I want to dedicate all
my Love with my heart mind body and soul to
the Man I fought so hard to come home to:

<u>Justin Alan Longwell</u>
I carried you with me in my heart till the day
that I came home.
Love you Forever and Always.

About The Author

I am currently 32 years of age. I grew up in Tampa where I was raised to be stupid and taught that I would never make anything of myself. Through my childhood and teen years I was bullied at school, home, and work.

In my Childhood and Adult life, I was severely mentally and emotionally abused which lead to years of unhappiness, cuttings and self mutilations, and several suicide attempts..my last being in 2010. I am going on 4 years of being Cut free, and Suicide is not an option for me any longer.

At 28-29, I went through an Awakening: or what the Bible calls *The Quickening*. I thought I had found my purpose in life: But here is the thing about God's will be done... The moment the spark of insanity hits, you cannot ask the student to provide you with a clear understanding of what is going on for even the student does not understand, so in the middle of Fighting for my Children in a DCF Custody battle I lost them: They deemed me mentally unstable, and I set out to do the impossible... To Prove them wrong.

Diary of A Mad Woman is A Journey that I will never forget...In the middle of my DCF battle, Diary of A Mad Woman wasn't even thought of...during my fight for my Children I was reevaluated by a Physiotherapist and Psychiatrist as having A mood disorder however not Bipolar because I knew how to deal with my emotions better than I once had and there was nothing wrong with me except I was smart as Hell...

So I was given the Idea to Journal my life events, and to write them down... Then a friend of mine, *Matt Yates*, suggested that I write a book, and from that moment Diary of a Mad Woman took form.

I had the vision of what I wanted for my life, and where I felt God wanted me... But I tell you dear Readers: Lean not on your own understanding but in all things ask for the understanding of the Higher power...

I am a completely changed person in Christ, fully understanding God's will for my life...And in the year to Follow I hope to have the *Journey Home* completed for all my Fans, Readers, Friends, and Family. For the *Journey Home* is the prayers I spoke for my Husband and Twin Flame, who I have now Found, and the adventures and battles that we will face together as one...

But the most Ironic part about the *Journey Home* is God led me Right back to the same place, and Home is where my Journey with God first begun in Canton, Ohio with my love *Justin Longwell*.

Author Angelica Warner